THE OPTIMIST SEES THE BAGEL,
THE PESSIMIST SEES THE HOLE

THE OPTIMIST SEES THE BAGEL

Leonard Sorcher

LIFE'S LITTLE JEWISH

THE PESSIMIST SEES THE HOLE

INSTRUCTION BOOK

POCKET BOOKS

New York   London   Toronto

Sydney   Tokyo   Singapore

POCKET BOOKS, a division of Simon & Schuster Inc.
1230 Avenue of the Americas, New York, NY 10020

Copyright © 1996 by Leonard Sorcher

ISBN: 0-671-00389-5

First Pocket Books hardcover printing December 1996

10   9   8   7   6   5   4   3   2   1

POCKET and colophon are registered trademarks of
Simon & Schuster Inc.

Designed by Stanley S. Drate/Folio Graphics Co. Inc.

Printed in Mexico

FOR MY MOTHER.

WHO ELSE?

MANY THANKS TO DAN COHEN; BETSY ELIAS;
DEBORAH YAFFE GREENWALD; MICHELE RAPKIN;
MY EDITOR, AMY EINHORN;
SOCRATES; BOO; PETEY; FAITH
AND MY VERY SPECIAL ANGEL, DIANA.

HE WHO LAUGHS, LASTS.

—*Anon*

The optimist
      sees the bagel,
the pessimist
      sees the hole.

If you can't say something nice, say it in Yiddish.

It's not who
you know,
it's who you know
had a nose job.

If it tastes good, it's probably not kosher.

After the destruction of
the Second Temple,
God created Loehmann's.

No one
looks good
in a yarmulke.

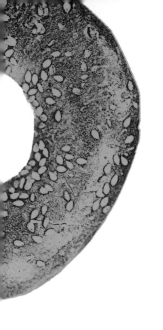

Who else
could have
invented
the 50-minute
hour?

Never pick your nose in *shul;* it's the one place you know He's watching.

Why spoil a good meal with a big tip?

WASPs leave
and never say
good-bye.
Jews say
good-bye
and never leave.

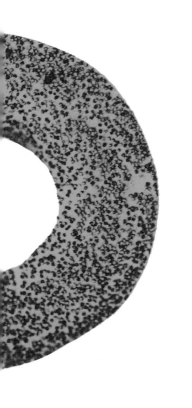

Twenty percent off is a bargain; fifty percent off is a *mitzvah*.

Wine needs
to breathe,
so don't rush
through the
kiddish.

Remember, even Sandy Koufax didn't play ball on Yom Kippur.

There's nothing
like a good belch.

Israel is the land
of milk and honey;
Florida is the land
of milk of magnesia.

Never pay retail.

It's always
a bad hair day
if you're bald.

Pork is forbidden,
but a pig in a blanket
makes a nice
hors d'oeuvre.

No one leaves
a Jewish wedding
hungry;
but then again,
no one leaves with
a hangover.

The High Holidays
have absolutely
nothing to do
with marijuana.

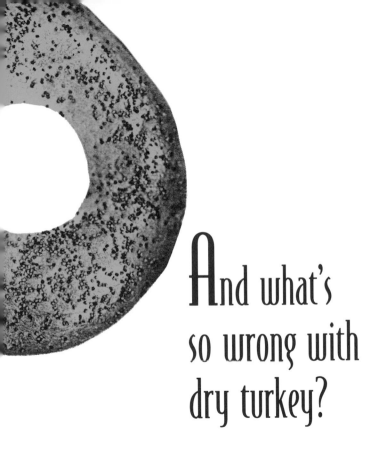

And what's
so wrong with
dry turkey?

If your name
was Lipschitz,
you'd change it,
too.

Always leave a little room
for the Viennese table.

Always
whisper
the names
of diseases.

One *mitzvah* can
change the world;
two will just make
you tired.

If you don't eat, it will kill me.

Anything worth saying
is worth repeating
a thousand times.

The most
important word
to know
in any language
is *sale.*

Where there's smoke, there may be smoked salmon.

Never take
a front-row
seat at a *bris.*

Prune danish
is definitely
an acquired taste.

Next year in Jerusalem. The year after that, how about a nice cruise?

Never leave
a restaurant
empty-handed.

Spring ahead, fall back,
winter in Miami Beach.

The important Jewish holidays are the ones on which alternate-side-of-the-street parking is suspended.

You need ten men for a *minyan*, but only four in polyester pants and white shoes for pinochle.

A bad matzoh
ball makes
a good
paperweight.

A *schmata*
is a dress that
your husband's ex
is wearing.

Without Jewish mothers, who would need therapy?

Before you read the menu, read the prices.

There comes a time in every man's life when he must stand up and tell his mother he's an adult. This usually happens at around age forty-five.

According to Jewish
dietary law,
pork and shellfish
may be eaten only
in Chinese restaurants.

Tsuris is a Yiddish word that means your child is marrying someone who isn't Jewish.

If you're going
to whisper at the movies,
make sure it's loud
enough for everyone
else to hear.

No meal
is complete
without
leftovers.

What business is a yenta in? Yours.

If you have to ask the price, you can't afford it. But if you can afford it, make sure you tell everybody what you paid.

The only thing
more important
than a good
education is
a good parking
spot at the mall.

Prozac is like chicken soup: it doesn't cure anything, but it makes you feel better.

Laugh now, but one day you'll be driving a big Cadillac and eating dinner at four in the afternoon.

Schmeer today,
gone tomorrow.

What is *chutzpah?*
Reading this entire book
in the store
and not buying it.

Leonard Sorcher is an advertising writer
who lives and works in New York City.